WATCHES

WATCHES

Grange
BOOKS

A QUANTUM BOOK

Published by Grange Books
an imprint of Grange Books Plc
The Grange
Kingsnorth Industrial Estate
Hoo, nr. Rochester
Kent ME3 9ND

1-84013-126-8

This book is produced by
Quantum Books Ltd
6 Blundell Street
London N7 9BH

Project Manager: Rebecca Kingsley
Project Editor: Judith Millidge
Designer: Wayne Humphries
Editor: Clare Haworth-Maden

The material in this publication previously appeared in
Classic Watch, Wristwatches

QUMTICS
Set in Times
Reproduced in Singapore by Eray Scan Pte Ltd
Printed in Singapore by Star Standard Industries (Pte) Ltd

CONTENTS

INTRODUCTION

Most of us wear one, and most of us believe that we couldn't do without one. We would be lost without a wristwatch to confirm the second in the minute in the hour in every day. It is said that as many people wear wristwatches as there are people wearing shoes on their feet, and the market for them is massive and ever expanding. The majority of this market is satisfied to wear an inexpensive, uncomplicated quartz digital or analogue watch on its wrist, just as long as it 'keeps time'. In recent years, however, the most interesting and unusual wristwatches have become recognised as collectable.

Left: Seiko's remarkable 'Speech Synthesiser'.

Above: The very first 'Mickey Mouse' watch, from 1933.

COUNTING THE HOURS

The only basis for measuring time in ancient days was the rotation of the earth and the apparent path of the sun from east to west across the sky. These were used by the first astronomers to divide the days and nights into regular units.

When humans ceased to be nomadic hunters and began to congregate into communities, they felt the need to split the day into something less vague than sunrise, noon and sunset. They noticed the difference in the length of the shadows cast by the sun, and they erected sticks and, later also larger edifices, whose shadows could be measured and related to the passage of time. One of the bigger structures is Cleopatra's Needle, which in 1500 BC stood outside a temple in Heliopolis in Egypt and now stands on the north bank of the river Thames in London. Some of these pillars were used to mark periods in the year – the Great Pyramid in Egypt, designed in part to determine the equinoxes, is an early example; so, too, is Stonehenge in England, erected around 1900 BC, where on Midsummer's Day, the sun rises over the heelstone at the time of the summer solstice.

Sometime in around 1000 BC appeared the

time-sticks of Egypt: T-shaped pieces of wood with raised crosspieces which cast a shadow on the long shaft, which was engraved to mark regular periods of time (the first 'hours'). It was placed facing east in the morning and had to be reversed to face west in the afternoon.

The time-stick was the forerunner of the sun dial, which is also believed to have originated in Egypt. A vertical bar called a gnomon casts a shadow on a horizontal dial. Later, the stick-like gnomon was replaced by an angled one pointing north and inclined according to the place of origin. Thus, the time could be told not by the length of shadow cast, but by its direction on the dial, a far more accurate process.

Another early device for measuring the passage of hours was the clepsydra, or water-clock. Said to have originated in China, where several different forms developed, it is also known to have been used in Babylon in around 1500 BC. An early type was also found at the Temple of Amon at Karnak in Egypt, which consisted of an alabaster bowl with rings and inscriptions on the outside and a small hole near the base. As the water escaped, the falling level could be made to show the hours. The outflow hole consisted of a drilled gemstone set into the alabaster – not unlike a jewelled bearing in a modern wristwatch.

But although water-clocks are not particularly handy objects, it was several centuries before their successors as time-keeping devices were developed. Sand, or hour, glasses first appeared in the 13th century; an early illustration shows two glass bulbs bound at the necks. A pierced diaphragm restricted the flow of sand from the upper to the lower bulb and,

Right: Cleopatra's Needle indicated the time by the shadows that it cast.

by measuring out the sand, the time taken could be controlled. These clocks could be easily made and, as well as being portable, they were furthermore more accurate time-keepers than the clepsydras.

Sand glasses were the industrial timers of the earliest factories and they were invaluable at sea, where, suspended from the ceiling, they operated well, even in rough seas. They were also a common sight on pulpits in churches. But they were counters: they told of the passage of time, they did not tell the time.

TELLING THE TIME

It is not precisely known when the mechanical clock, the first instrument used for actually telling the time, was invented. Early clocks usually only had one hand and were called *horloges,* from the Roman name for a water-clock – *horlogium*; that with a bell for tolling the hours was called a *clocca*. Quite large, these were usually made for churches, where they stood on the floor, but later models were installed in towers.

When dials and hands were added to the church clocks, the mechanism used to display the times of day was often separate from the striking part, and was called the 'watch'. These tower clocks were driven by weights, and it was not until a coiled spring was introduced as the source of power that smaller clocks became a practical proposition.

DOMESTIC CLOCKS

Now began the era of the domestic clocks, the first of which were probably the lantern clocks used by watchmen, who hung them on hooks on the wall when not in use. Soon they mer-

Left: The ancient clock in Salisbury Cathedral, England.

ited a permanent place on the wall, and it became fashionable to build wooden cases around them and to mount them on brackets. By 1600 they were being made of brass instead of iron; this had the effect of making them smaller still, and moved them out of the province of the blacksmith and into the hands of the skilled clockmaker.

Around 1657, the Dutch astronomer and physicist Christiaan Huygens devised his novel pendulum clock, and the idea was enthusiastically embraced by English clockmakers led by Ahasuerus Fromanteel, the first to obtain the right to use the pendulum.

The next step in the evolution of the domestic clock came with the rich traveller in his carriage who wished to know the time. These so-called 'carriage clocks', which the

Above: Spring clock by John Drew, London, late 17th century.

Right: Musical clock by Jacquet Droz, c.1770. A fine red Boulle pendule, complete with orginal bracket. Both case and bracket have fine ormolu mounts.

French became especially skilled at making, were mainly of brass, and were housed in rectangular cases. These clocks frequently incorporated repeating striking mechanisms so that the owner could tell the time of day by pressing a knob on the top.

GREENWICH MEAN TIME

If timepieces are to be really accurate, they have to be related to some common, agreed point – a timely benchmark. Thanks to the work of English clockmakers, work on ship's chronometers was carried to greater lengths. Good time-keeping at sea was essential for accurate navigation and also for cartography, but making a clock that could tolerate the pitching of a ship at sea was a major undertaking,

Above: Two-day chronometer by Parkinson & Frodsham, Change Alley, London, No 3234, c.1850. A mid-19th-century marine chronometer typical of the thousands used by the navies of the world between 1820 and 1950.

Right: Two-day chronometer by Brockbank and Atkins, No 1159, London, c.1870. A two-day chronometer suspended on gimbals. The movement was kept level, even in rough seas.

The time ball at Greenwhich Observatory, first installed in 1833.

and one which demanded new technologies. John Harrison (1693–1776) finally overcame this problem, but it was left to other clock-makers, like John Arnold and Thomas Earnshaw, to make Harrison's invention of the marine chronometer a practical proposition, simplifying its production so that it could be made in quantity without losing any of its accuracy. These chronometers are contained in three-tiered wooden boxes, supported on brass gimbals, so that whatever the movement of the ship, the clock remains horizontal. A Frenchman, Pierre Le Roy, contributed the compensated balance which was made of two

Right: Invented in 1795 and patented in 1805, the tourbillon device remains the most familiar of Abraham-Louis Breguet's many inventions.

English clockmaker Thomas Tompion (1639–1713).

John Harrison (1693–1776), a leading English clockmaker.

dissimilar metals to overcome the effects of temperature changes, and by the 19th century marine chronometers had achieved a high degree of accuracy. But there still remained the need for some sort of time signal by which they could be set.

John Pond, the Astronomer Royal, solved the problem in 1833 by installing a time ball at Greenwich Observatory. This was a wooden ball about 10 feet (3m) in diameter, which slid up and down a 15-foot-high (4.5m) mast. Just before 1pm each day, the ball was wound up to the top of the mast and at 1pm precisely it was dropped by a trigger mechanism. Later, an electrical device was connected so

that the observatory's mean solar time clock could release it automatically. Time balls were subsequently installed at all the major ports, and there was even one erected in the Strand in London so that the clockmakers who worked there could set their chronometers.

But different towns were still keeping to different local times, so, in 1880, mean solar time at Greenwich was legally established as Britain's official time. In 1884 an international conference decided to adopt the meridian through Greenwich as zero, and to use Greenwich Mean Time as the basis for a global system. The world was divided into 24 time zones, each one an hour apart; only Ireland

The Swiss watchmaker Abraham-Louis Breguet, born 1747.

and France opposed the proposition, which was nevertheless adopted.

Electricity was a boon to the distribution of time: Big Ben was linked to Greenwich by the electric telegraph for time checks, as was the Post Office, still a vital link today in the supply of time. Shortly after World War I, an American named Henry Ellis Warren invented the synchronous clock which he called the Telechron. It operated from the main electricity supply – and to that extent was only as accurate as the stability of the frequency – but it was another step forward, although strictly speaking it was not a clock but an electric motor. In Britain, the firm of S Smith & Sons took up the idea and became the biggest manufacturer of synchronous clocks. Unfortunately, World War II caused fluctuations in electricity supply and affected sales for many years. It was not until the mid-1950s that mains electricity would be stable enough for people to trust synchronous clocks again.

But an alternative had already appeared. Both the French and German clock industries had been working on battery clocks. One version, designed by Kienzle, was an ordinary mechanical clock with a light main spring which was rewound every 15 minutes by a battery operating on a solenoid. The system provided a relatively constant drive and therefore good time-keeping. Such clocks were ideal in the house as they required little attention, and they were also quickly adopted for use in automobiles as dashboard clocks since battery power was readily available. Both Kienzle and Smith developed automotive subsidiaries that are still in existence today.

With the invention of the transistor in 1948, electric clocks became even more reliable, but the chief effect was to point the way to the development of the electronic time-keeper.

ELECTRONIC REVOLUTION

The first electronic timepiece ever produced was built by W A Morrison in 1929 and was about the size of a small room! The clock was based on the principle that a piece of quartz crystal, cut in a certain way, will resonate at a certain frequency if an electric current is applied to it. In other words, the crystal behaves like an extremely rapidly vibrating balance wheel. A subsequent development of this was the atomic clock, based on the vibrations of an atom of cesium, which are several million times faster than those of a quartz crystal. Said to be accurate to within one second in 3,000 years, a radioactive cesium clock is rather impractical for everyday use, but it is the basis for National Time in Britain and elsewhere, as the signals are used for accurate international time-setting and for navigational purposes. Britain broadcasts time signals from the Post Office clock at Rugby and the United States of America from Fort Collins in Colorado. Other transmitters are located in Nagasaki in Japan and Frankfurt in Germany.

THE PERSONAL TIMEPIECE: THE WATCH

In 1511, a young German locksmith named Peter Henlein built the first really portable personal time-keeper using a small coiled spring – much as he used in his locks- and a scaled-down train of gears. They called it the 'Nuremberg Egg', and this time-keeper, now called a watch, was to inspire craftsmen all over Europe but especially in Geneva, where a flood of refugees from France and Germany – many of whom were watch- and clockmakers – were fleeing from religious persecution and sought refuge in the free city, and to whose inhabitants they taught their craft.

Watchmaking soon became one of Switzerland's most important industries, spreading eastwards along the Jura mountains as far as La Chaux de Fonds and Neufchatel. Some of these early watches were wound by a key through their one hand (clocks with two hands had only been in existence for about 25 years) and had a bow at 12 o'clock through which passed the ribbon or chain on which they were suspended. At this stage, in 1675, Christiaan Huygens, the man who had invented the pendulum clock, introduced the spiral hairspring, which made for greater accuracy and facilitated the introduction of the minute hand. It was about this time, too, that men's fashions dictated the wearing of the waistcoat: what was more natural than to slip one's watch into a waistcoat pocket instead of hanging it around one's neck?

The next hundred years was the golden age of English horology, which saw the work of some of the greatest clockmakers of all time, most of whom were equally at home making watches. They included Robert Hooke (1635–1703), Thomas Tompion (1639–1713), George Graham (1673–1751), John Harrison (1693–1776) and Thomas Mudge (1715–94).

Mudge had been working on the idea for an anchor escapement for watches similar to that used so successfully in pendulum clocks. In 1759 he made first a bracket clock, and then a watch with a lever escapement, said to be the most important invention in watchmaking after the balance spring.

Another far-reaching development then took place. Up till then, the pivots of the train had run in metal bearings, which resulted in wear and loss of accuracy. A Swiss clockmaker,

An original Abraham-Louis Perrelet watch, from the Beyer Museum. The watchmaking origins of the Perrelet family go back to the early years of the 18th century.

living in England, conceived the idea of using a ruby as the bearing, both at the ends of the pivots and pierced as a bearing in the plate. The technique was adopted with great enthusiasm by the English, but they kept it to themselves. It vastly improved the smooth running of the watches, and thus their accuracy.

Switzerland, too, had its innovative watchmakers, and foremost among them was Abraham-Louis Breguet (1747–1823), whose contributions to horology include the self-winding watch – an invention first conceived by Abraham-Louis Perrelet around 1770; a shock protection system; and the tourbillon, a device to offset the effects of gravity on a watch's performance.

From the last quarter of the 18th century to the end of the 19th century, pocket watches became more and more sophisticated. Specialist firms which only made certain parts grew up; others concentrated on the movements; while a third group, often known as *etablisseurs*, assembled the various components into complete watches.

The period also saw the founding of some of Switzerland's great houses, headed by Vacheron Constantin in 1755, Blancpain, Jaeger-LeCoultre, Longines, Cartier and IWC (The International Watch Co), which belonged to the elite band of producers known as manufacturers who made every part of their watches, including the movements, themselves.

Watches became more complicated, incorporating repeaters, phases of the moon, perpetual calendars and chronographs, but they still tended to be rather bulky, with their movements protected by double cases (which were known as 'hunters') which had a hinged cover over the glass. Then came a development that was to change the design of the personal timekeeper forever: the wristwatch.

Below left: The logos of the great Swiss watchmaking houses.

Below right: A Grande complication *hunter watch from 1889.*

THE
WRISTWATCH

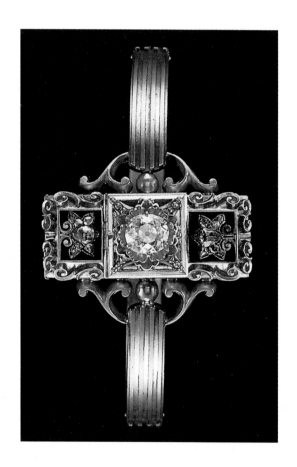

Just when the wristwatch was invented and by whom is not clear. Company archives show that Breguet made a watch for the Queen of Naples in 1810: watch No 2639 was 'designed to be worn on the wrist'. Patek Philippe had created a watch with a diameter of only 8.46mm (0.3in) for the Great Exhibition at the Crystal Palace in London in 1851, and then in 1868 the firm made a wristwatch for Countess Kosewicz based on the earlier design. It was to be some fifty years however, before the company produced a commercially viable model.

Above: The Cartier 'Santos-Dumont' watch.

Previous page: The first wristwatch – made for Countess Kosewicz in 1868.

In 1886 Girard Perregaux received an order for watches for the officers of the Imperial German Navy, and in 1904 Louis Cartier produced a wristwatch for his friend Alberto Santos-Dumont, a Brazilian aviator, in response to a request for a timepiece that was more convenient than any currently available to use when piloting his airship. By the early 1900s, a number of firms were engaged in wristwatch production, but all were rather expensive, mainly because there was such a large amount of hand-craftsmanship involved in making the watches

WATCHES FOR THE MASSES

It is largely due to some American manufacturers that wristwatches were made available to ordinary people. Around 1850, a group of American watch companies got together with the idea of making a time-keeper for the masses. After the Industrial Revolution, machinery had become much more sophisticated, and the idea was to make thousands of identical, interchangeable parts which could be assembled by cheap labour, an idea later used by Henry Ford to produce his famous Model T motorcars. After several false starts, the Waterbury Clock Company succeeded in producing a watch that sold for $3.50, but its main

ambition was to get the price down to $1.

The first man to achieve this aim was Robert Ingersoll who, with his brother Charles, ran a mail-order business where every item in their catalogue was priced at $1. Ingersoll persuaded the Waterbury Clock Company to make him a small clock movement by giving it an order – quite considerable in those days – for 12,000 units. These were housed in a case that Ingersoll designed himself, and the first models, with a chain, sold for $1.50. They were so successful that Ingersoll went back to Waterbury with an order for half a million pieces, and these he sold for just $1. Ingersoll had reached his ambition to sell a watch for a day's pay, and christened his product 'The watch that made the dollar famous'.

By the early 1900s the line included a petite ladies' model called the 'Midget'. When the demand came for inexpensive wristwatches for the armed forces, it was easy to solder a pair of wire lugs at 12 o'clock and 6 o'clock and run a strap across the back. Thus the world's first inexpensive wristwatch was born. It still had the crown at the top, but when that was moved to the 3 o'clock position on the case, it looked just like its more expensive counterparts! Ingersoll's other innovation was to devise a form of luminous paint, which was applied to the hands and the numerals so that the soldiers could see the time in the dark. He named his invention 'Radiolite', but subsequently the use of radium compounds was banned on heath grounds.

MASS-PRODUCED WRISTWATCHES

The concept of using machinery to make accurate and interchangeable parts was not confined to inexpensive watches. Many of the prestigious Swiss companies took up the idea and improved the quantity and extent of their output without jeopardising quality, since all the parts were still meticulously assembled by hand. The English watchmakers, on the other hand, refused to have anything to do with these ideas, and consequently the English watchmaking industry went into a decline, one from which it has never recovered.

England had previously had a thriving watchmaking industry in the middle of the 19th century, with centres at Liverpool, Coventry and London. In 1858, the British Horological Institute was founded to protect the interests of its clock- and watchmaking members, largely against foreign competition. They were aware of the American ideas of mass production and knew that European companies were following suit, but the British craftsmen continued to complain about competition from cheap labour while not realising that the future lay in increasing mechanisation. Watchmaking in Britain was still largely dominated by craft traditions whose

Above: Robert Ingersoll, creator of 'The watch that made the dollar famous'.

Founded 1858

Above: Logo of the British Horological Institute, founded in 1858 to protect its members.

Left: The original Ingersoll 'Dollar' watch.

Right: The world's first inexpensive wristwatch, from Ingersoll.

RÉPUBLIQUE ET CANTON DE
NEUCHATEL (SUISSE)
·   ·

OBSERVATOIRE ASTRONOMIQUE
ET CHRONOMÉTRIQUE

BULLETIN DE MARCHE

Le soussigné certifie que le chronomètre N° — 681 —

diamètre: 25.5 mm   échappement: ancre à cheville
spiral: Nivarox   balancier: monométallique

de

ORIS WATCH Co., S.A.,

H O L S T E I N   a subi les épreuves pour

CHRONOMÈTRES-BRACELET

conformément au règlement (voir au verso) et a donné les résultats suivants :

Ecart moyen de la marche diurne . . . . E = + 0.20
Coefficient thermique . . . . C = - 0.022
Erreur secondaire de la compensation . . . . S = + 3.21
Reprise de marche (périodes 1 et 10) . . . . R = + 0.20
Variation des marches moyennes du plat au pendu . . . . - 0.73
Variation des marches moyennes du cadran en haut au cadran en bas . . - 0.72
Ecart moyen correspondant à un changement de position . . . . P = + 1.65

Neuchâtel,.. le 30 avril 1968

Le directeur de l'Observatoire,

Les chronomètres sont comparés tous les jours à l'horloge fondamentale
de l'Observatoire, au moyen d'un chronographe-enregistreur.
Le signe + indique l'avance, le signe — le retard.

practitioners failed to realise that the competition had moved on.

It was apparent to the Swiss that the secret lay in the quality of the machine tools that were to be used. Many firms already employed engineers of the highest calibre. Georges-August Lechot, for example, had designed and built a range of machines for Vacheron Constantin that revolutionised the firm's production as far back as 1843. But because the majority of Swiss watches at that time were of the better-quality, jewelled-lever variety, they were still relatively inexpensive.

THE ROSKOPF WATCH

American companies were not the only ones to have considered the possibilities of making a cheap watch for the masses. In the middle of the 19th century, a German watchmaker named Georges-Frederic Roskopf, who was working in La Chaux de Fonds, decided that he could make a watch for 20 francs. He set about simplifying the escapement mechanism by eliminating a number of parts and replacing the jewels in the lever with pins. He also modified the winding and made the cases less expensive. Much to the amazement of the industry, Roskopf received a bronze medal at the 1868 Paris Exhibition. One hundred years later, the Swiss were still exporting 28 million 'Roskopf' watches a year, and were the leading supplier of cheap watches.

At first, the traditional watchmakers did not think much of Roskopf's watches – initially, many were of poor manufacture – but as production became more refined, pin-lever watches achieved a respectable quality in relation to their price. One Swiss manufacturer, Oris,

Left: An official certificate of 'Chronometer' quality.

entered pin-lever watches in an official trial and received a certificate of chronometer quality, much to the chagrin of the jewel-lever watchmaking fraternity!

SELF-WINDING WRISTWATCHES

In 1923 John Harwood produced the first self-winding wristwatch. The system had originally been devised by Perrelet for pocket watches in 1770, but in spite of the popularity of the wristwatch, no one had previously thought of applying the principle to them. With no English manufacturer to take up his idea, Harwood patented it in Switzerland, where it was quickly adopted, most notably by the Rolex Watch Company, which was in production with a perpetual, self-winding wristwatch by 1931.

By the 1960s the watch industry in the middle and upper price ranges was virtually dominated by the Swiss, who could be forgiven for thinking that the watch had reached its zenith. Firms like Audemars Piguet, International Watch Co and Patek Philippe were creating complicated timepieces with a multiplicity of functions, hand-finished to an incredible degree of accuracy and housed in fabulous, 18-carat-gold cases which were engraved and embellished with precious gems. What more could one want in a watch? The exciting answer was not far away.

RADIO-CONTROLLED TIME

In the 1980s a German firm, Junghans, developed a radio-controlled clock which operated from time signals transmitted from the national transmitters located in Rugby in England, Fort Collins in Colorado, USA, Nagasaki in Japan and Frankfurt in Germany. These signals included both time and date information, so that adjustment for leap years, short months and seasonal time changes were

Left: The Rolex self-wind. The movement is wound by the slightest action of the wrist.

Below: An advertisement from 1929 for the remarkable invention by Englishman John Harwood in 1924 of the self-winding watch mechanism, patented in Switzerland.

made automatically. In the Junghans' clock, the receiver was activated every hour. The firm's next innovation was to cram all this cutting-edge technology into a wristwatch with the reception antenna hidden in the strap. The time measured by the 'Mega' wristwatch series is corrected once a day, and since the seconds' display is digital – and that is usually all that will ever need to be corrected – the system is even simpler than that used for the clocks, with their hourly correction.

THE ELECTRIC WATCH

In 1952, Fred Lip, a French watch manufacturer, produced the prototype of a watch powered by a battery. Working with the Elgin Company of America, Lip tried to manufacture them, but few were actually produced. The first genuinely electronic watch incorporating a transistorised circuit was designed by a Swiss engineer, Max Hetzel. But finding no support in his idea in his own country, he took it to Bulova in the United States,

A Junghans 'Mega' radio-controlled watch.

which marketed it. It was called the 'Tuning Fork', because the shape of the oscillator was so shaped.

A number of Swiss manufacturers then banded together to finance the research and development of a quartz oscillator. The Centre for Electric Horology in Neufchatel produced the first quartz-based movement: called 'Beta I', it won first prize in a competition organised by the centre, with a prototype from Seiko taking second place.

Seiko was no stranger to the technology, having already produced a large quartz chronometer to time the Olympic Games in 1964. In 1968 the firm entered a wristwatch version for the centre's competition, and the following year launched the first commercially viable quartz wristwatch, the 'Astron'.

DIGITAL DISPLAYS

Meanwhile, in the United States, a number of large companies already involved in the space programme had developed calculator modules to display digital time. An obvious disadvantage was that, in order to see the time, the user had to press a button on the side of the case. To obviate this, Ebauches SA in Switzerland and Texas Instruments in

Above: The Junghans 'Mega' picks up the time signal from Frankfurt, Germany, once a day, and features automatic setting for summer and winter.

Right: The Seiko 'Astron' watch, dating from c.1969.

California joined forces to develop the LCD, the liquid crystal display, whose readout was permanently visible. The problem was that both these systems drained the energy given out by their tiny batteries very rapidly.

In Switzerland and Japan, companies concentrated on producing watches with 'normal' faces – with a dial and hands – and by using stepping motors translated the vibrations of the quartz crystal into rotary motion to turn the hands. The 'analogue' system became the universal one for the better-quality timepieces.

The outstanding aspect of the new watches was their incredible accuracy – but they still had the drawback of having to have their batteries replaced, even though the latest type of lithium batteries can last for up to ten years. So the two firms decided to do away with batteries altogether. The Seiko 'Kinetic' model, launched in 1993 after twenty years of development, employs a tiny rotor, much like the mechanical automatic, which uses the wearer's movements to generate electricity into a specially designed capacitor which acts as a reservoir, storing power until it is needed. It is so efficient that, once it is fully charged, the watch will operate for 14 days without being worn.

SOLAR TECHNOLOGY

An entirely different system is embodied in the Citizen 'Eco-Drive', which uses advanced ceramics on the dial that allows light to pass through: light falls on a photo-electric cell which converts it into energy. It gains enough energy from one minute of daylight or 15 minutes of artificial light to run the watch for 24 hours. The energy is stored in a secondary battery which releases the power as required and, once fully charged, the watch will then run for between two and six months, depending

Above: The Seiko 'Kinetic SQ100' offers quartz accuracy along with the convenience of batteries.

Citizen's 'Eco-Drive Slim', a quartz battery watch that is barely three-sixteenths of an inch in cross-section.

This tourbillon with three gold bridges won Girard-Perregaux two gold medals at the Paris Exposition Universelle in 1867 and again in 1889.

on the model, without having to be exposed again to light.

In a further refinement, Junghans, which had also been developing solar technology, combined this with the radio system in its 'Mega-Solar-Ceramic' model. The case is made from zirconium oxide ceramic, with the antenna placed in it; the solar system, when fully charged – which takes 30 minutes of bright light – will run for up to six months, even in darkness and is corrected, like the original 'Mega' watch, by the nearest national radio transmitter. So, the wheel has come neatly full circle, and the sun, which first allowed ancient people to mark the passage of time, now operates the most technologically advanced electronic timepieces.

TYPES OF WATCHES

A mechanical watch consists of three elements: the source of power – the main spring; a series of toothed wheels – the train – which transmits the power; and a regulating mechanism comprising a balance wheel, a hair spring and an escapement. Mechanical watches have either a jewelled-lever or pin-lever escapement – a variation of the latter is the Roskopf escapement used mainly in cheaper productions. The escapement is located between an oscillator – the balance wheel – and the gear-train. The lever version was invented by Thomas Mudge and remains virtually the same today as in his.

The crown (the winder) winds the main spring; as it unwinds, the toothed rim of its casing (the barrel) sets in motion the wheels of the train, which act on the hands to show the time. The most important part of this operation is controlling the transmission of power so that it is even and regular.

For reliably accurate measurement, time

must be divided into absolutely equal parts; the briefer they are, the more precise the measurement. The balance wheel rotates a half-revolution in one way before being pulled up by the hair spring at its centre, when it then rotates in the opposite direction. The oscillation effectively chops the action into equal parts and creates the familiar tick-tock sound of mechanical watches. These half-oscillations are called vibrations, and are known as the beat; a normal watch beats as 18,000 vibrations per hour, while a very high-frequency movement has 36,00 vph.

Each movement of the balance wheel acts

Above: The leader of the field of mechanical chronographs, the Breitling 'Chronomat' has been improved and modified since its initial launch.

Right: A Grande complication *from the firm of Audemars Piguet.*

on an anchor-shaped lever, which frees one tooth at a time of the escape wheel. Thus the power of the main spring is turned into a rhythmic series of movements, which ultimately end up, via the reduction gears, at the hands to show the time.

Wherever friction occurs, jewels are fitted. Originally, the jewels were rubies, but are now man-made corundum. The jewels of a jewel-lever watch are situated at the ends of the lever; in a pin-lever, they are replaced completely by hardened-steel pins.

An ordinary mechanical watch has around 130 parts, which are situated between the bottom plate and the bridges which keep them together. Movements come in various sizes, which are measured in millimetres or lignes,

where 1 ligne = 2.25mm. To distinguish movements of the same size but by different makers, the word calibre is always used.

Automatic watches are operated by the action of a rotor, which winds the watch through the wearer's movements. The advantage to this is that in addition to not having to wind the watch each day, the main spring is kept fully wound, so the power output, and thus the rate of the watch, is constant.

CHRONOGRAPHS

Chronographs, or stopwatches, are watches with a stop/start facility which enables the wearer to time an event and count the lapsed time in seconds, minutes and hours. The mechanism is operated by a slide or knob on the side of the case. A rattrapante (or flyback) chronograph has two centre second hands which can be operated separately in order to time two competitors at once. Most chronographs time to 1/5th second; the main mechanism keeps running when the centre second hands fly back to zero.

CHRONOMETERS

Chronometers are very high-quality watches which have undergone stringent individual tests at the official testing station, the Controle Official Suisse des Chronometres. Only when it passes the test is a watch awarded its certificate of quality.

Phases of the moon are astronomically predictable, as are leap years, and so they can be programmed into a watch mechanism. Provided it is not stopped, the watch can run into the next century.

GRANDE COMPLICATIONS

Grande complications are pocket or wristwatches which combine telling the time with

Above: Seiko's remarkable 'Speech Synthesiser': a digital quartz with both a recording and playback facility in four or eight seconds, chronograph, alarm, automatic month, day and date calendar and an illumination light.

Left: The 'Datalink' from Timex includes easy-to-use software to store up to 70 personal reminders.

Above: The logo of ETA Fabrique d'Ebauches at Grenchen. The 200-year-old company turns out 100 million movements a year, three-quarters of which are quartz.

Right: Advertisement for the Ingersoll 'Radiolite' watch, c.1915.

every known function: perpetual calendars, moon phases, stop/start mechanisms, alarms, repeaters, strikes and even thermometers. A typical example from Patek Philippe is an astronomical pocket watch, with a tourbillon escapement which has 33 functions, 1,728 parts and which took four years to assemble!

ELECTRONIC WATCHES

Like its mechanical counterpart, the electronic watch has a power source, a regulator, and a system to display the time, either digitally or by means of hands and a dial. The power source is a battery, and its current is conveyed to an integrated circuit – the regulator – which accepts the vibrations of a quartz oscillator and transforms them into impulses which conform to an agreed frequency – now universally accepted as 32,768 Hertz, or vibrations per second. Because electronic oscillations are very much of a higher order than those of a mechanical balance, which at a maximum is 36,000 vph, it became necessary to devise a new standard. The Hertz, corresponding to one vibration per second, was therefore adopted. Impulses are either fed into a steeping motor which drives a chain of gears to activate the hands, or processed by the integrated circuit-driver section to command an LCD (liquid crystal display).

The batteries used today are silver oxide, or the longer-lasting lithium types. Analogue models usually need only one battery, which can last from two to five and even ten years, depending on the model.

The oscillator is a piezoelectric quartz crystal cut by laser to an exact, predetermined shape to give the required frequency of 32,768 Hz. The integrated circuit (IC) is more often than not of the CMOS-LS type. The stepping motor transforms the impulses from the driver part

Above: The Timex 'Indiglo', which illuminates time using electroluminescence.

of the IC into a rotating or rocking motion. Original motors were only capable of driving the hands and date display; modern complicated quartz watches employ up to four stepping motors in order to drive their multiple functions. Sometimes, solar cells are fitted into quartz watches to transform light into electrical energy, which can then be stored in an accumulator in the watch.

LIQUID CRYSTALS

Liquid crystals combine a liquid and a solid state. Elongated molecules arranged parallel to each other can be switched from vertical to horizontal positions by stimulation from an electric current – like a Venetian blind being opened and closed. The vertical molecules are transparent and admit light; the horizontal molecules are opaque and reflect light, with the reflection appearing as a black area. The liquid crystals are layered between very thin glass plates bearing a grid of electrodes which form the seven segments needed to form the digits 0 to 9. The driver section of the IC determines which segments are to be activated, in what order and for how long, in order to form the appropriate digits.

The variety of functions (which are really programmes) provided by digital watches involves far more complicated ICs than those found in analogue quartz watches, and some modern digital models now even incorporate a microprocessor!

MOVEMENTS

Apart from the elite Swiss firms, which make their own movements, most watch manufacturers buy their movements from specialist firms, the largest of which is ETA Fabrique d'Ebauches at Grenchen. This 200-year-old company is now part of SMH (Societe Suisse

*The flagship line from IWC, the Mark XII
'Flieger-Chronograph'.*

de Microelectronique et d'Horlogerie), and
owns factories in Switzerland, France,
Germany, Malaysia and Taiwan. It turns out
100 million movements each year, three quarters of which are quartz. The movements come
in a series of 'families' based on size, quality or price. Its mechanical movements are of
high quality, a typical example being the Valjou
7750 chronograph movement.

ETA's movements, both quartz and mechanical, are also supplied to the 'house brands'
of SMH – Omega, Longines, Rado and Tissot.

Other sources of movements in Switzerland
are Ronda, an old-established family firm in
Lengnau, and ISA, which specialises in ultra-
thin quartz movements for the top end of the
watch trade. The big Japanese firms not only
make their own movements, but also supply
them to other selected manufacturers.

FEATURES

As a result of the demand from the army during World War I, the dials and hands of watches were often painted with luminous substances
so the wearer could tell the time in the dark.
The early luminous substances often contained
zinc sulphide, which was activated by a radioactive salt. This potentially dangerous material was banned in the 1950s and has now been
replaced by tritium, a substance of low ra-
dioactivity, the amount of which is carefully mon-
itored and controlled by ISO standards.

LIGHTING-UP TIME

Recently, other means of illuminating the time
have been devised: the Timex 'Indiglo' system is based on electroluminescence. By pressing a button on the side of the case, a minute
current from the battery is activated, which
excites electrodes on the dial which then give
off energy in the form of light. An alternative

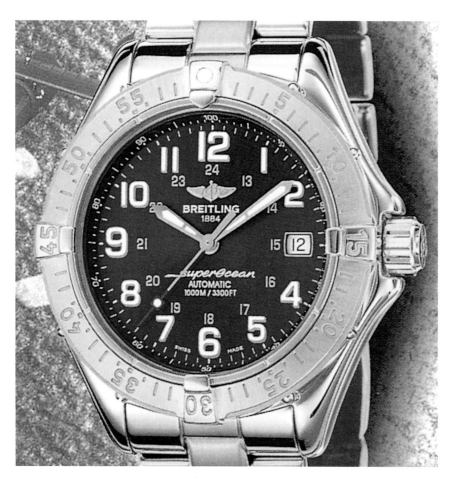

The Breitling Colt 'Superocean' in 18-carat gold. The case is tough enough to withstand underwater pressures equivalent to 3,300ft (1,006m).

The latest ETA movement incorporates a power-reserve indicator as a matter of course. Now also universal is shock protection, and most good watches use Incabloc, a system derived from Breguet's original parachut. In order to be called shockproof, a watch must meet the conditions set out in the International Standard 1413, which includes two blows on the case which are equivalent to a 1 metre (3.3ft) drop onto a hard surface. After that, the watch must not show a variation in rate of more than 60 seconds per day.

ANTI-MAGNETISM

Most watches now claim to be anti-magnetic. A mechanical watch can be thrown off balance if it comes into contact with a strong magnetic field – something that is very common in everyday life, since magnets are to be found in automobiles, hi-fi systems and even refrigerators. To overcome the effects, alloys are used for the balance wheel, escape wheel and other parts. But a watch can only be described as anti-magnetic if it does not stop after exposure to a magnetic field of 4900 amps per meter and subsequently does not deviate by more than 30 seconds per day. While the majority of better-class watches certainly qualify, if a wearer does need special protection then a watch like the IWC' Ingenieur' is called for. Its movement is housed in a complete alloy jacket inside the normal case, and even the dial is made of anti-magnetic soft iron.

Alternatively, an electronic watch would be suitable, since it is not susceptible to magnetism and because it has fewer parts than a mechanical watch and no balance staff; neither does it need special shockproof devices.

WATER-RESISTANCE

Today, most watches are water-resistant. This

system has the dial coated with fluorescent material which is activated after a short period of exposure to any source of light, after which it will last for another eight hours.

POWER AND SHOCK

The idea of having an indication of the power remaining in the main spring was, in fact, first devised by Breguet in the late 18th century, and has appeared in various guises ever since.

is the only accepted description, since the term 'waterproof' is no longer allowed internationally. The patents protecting the original screwdown crowns have long since expired, and accurate machining means that cases can be made to be relatively water-resistant. But to go underwater to great depths presents another set of serious problems that require special gaskets and even helium valves, as in the Breitling 'Superocean'. Watches which are used by divers at depths of 100 feet (30.5m) or more need to be checked regularly and have their gaskets replaced. The main advantage of water-resistance, however, is that it also keeps out the main enemy of all delicate mechanisms – dust!

CRYSTAL CLEAR

The crystal, often still called the glass – even though ordinary glass has not been used for many years – is now made from acrylic plastic, a rugged compound that does not yellow with age and can be cut, moulded or injected, or mineral glass, a natural glass which has been chemically treated to form a tempered hard outer coating which is resistant to knocks and scratches. The very best watches, however, have sapphire crystals, manmade corundums, but with the hardness of real sapphires. To all intents and purposes, crystals of corundum are scratchproof. They are especially used to make the transparent backs of complicated watches.

A gentleman's dress 'skeleton' model, showing traditional mechanical movements.

18TH- AND 19TH-CENTURY WATCHMAKERS

In 1988, according to a survey carried out by Citizen, some 653 million wristwatches of all types were manufactured. A wristwatch makes a statement about its wearer. It is not a necessary adornment, and yet it is commonly worn by both men and women. It is bought with great care and forethought, whether for the purchaser or for someone else, out of duty or love. An image of the wearer has to be summoned up and, with luck, matched to the shape, design, color, functions, and the cost of an exquisite machine, which may be worn and consulted daily for decades to come.

BLANCPAIN

In the remarkable history of watchmakers, Blancpain stands out as being the oldest. Jehan-Jacques Blancpain's name first appeared on a watch in 1735. His "factory" was, in fact, a large farmhouse in Villaret in the Vallée de Joux, and it was another hundred years before his great-grandson managed to build a small factory in which to make the complete watches that were acquiring a reputation in France, Germany, and Russia. The business continued to pass from father to son through 13 generations, until the death of Frederic-Emil Blancpain in 1932 marked the end of the Blancpain dynasty. For the next 40 years the firm was run by Madame Fichter, and the company name changed to Rayville (a close anagram of Villaret).

In the meantime, in 1926, the company went into production with the world's first self-winding wristwatch, based on John Harwood's patented design. In 1953 a diver's watch, water-resistant to a depth of 660 feet (183m) caused a stir when worn by the underwater adventurer Jacques Cousteau, and later became the standard issue for the French Navy. Then came the "Ladybird," the most compact watch movement ever seen – a mere 5 lignes (11.85mm) in diameter. But, as with many watchmaking

Previous page: A selection of classic watches auctioned at Sotheby's in London, England, in 1988.

Above: The "Ladybird," with automatic movement, from Blancpain.

companies, the advent of quartz seriously affected the firm, and it was taken over by a consortium of manufacturers, including Omega, the name falling into disuse.

In 1983, 250 years after it was first founded, Blancpain was back under its new owners, however, and, in a farmhouse in Le Brassus, a building nearly identical to the one in which the founder had worked, the Blancpain headquarters were established. The occasion was marked by the launch of an automatic wristwatch with a perpetual calendar, with the innovation of displaying the phases of the Moon. The six great masterpieces in wristwatch-making – the chronometer, minute repeater, Moonphase calendar, perpetual calendar, tourbillon regulator, and ultrathin chronometer – are all made by Blancpain. It has never used quartz movements and never will; its watches are distinguishable by the movements listed above and

the materials they incorporate: 18-carat gold (which may be pink, white, or yellow), platinum and 18-carat gold with steel, with or without precious stones, hand-sewn leather straps (interchangeable with metal bracelets), dial indicators in 18-carat gold, and scratch-resistant sapphire crystals. The total output is some 6000 watches a year, all the parts of which are assembled, polished, and finished by 15 watchmakers. Each watch is numbered on the movement and case and signed for in the register. There is only one shape and basic design of case – round – and only two sizes – ladies' and gentlemen's – but there is a choice of dials, as long as they are white with Roman numerals!

VACHERON CONSTANTIN

Vacheron Constantin has been in uninterrupted watch production since 1755, when it began to build its reputation for making watches of

Above: An automatic perpetual-calendar watch by Blancpain, in stainless steel with a Moon-phase aperture.

Above left: The only tourbillon with a power reserve of eight days – perfection in miniature from Blancpain.

the highest quality. Founded by Jean-Marc Vacheron, the firm passed to Barthelemy Vacheron at the end of the century, who took into partnership François Constantin. To meet the demand for their goods, they employed a mechanical genius name Lechot, who designed and built a range of precision machines which revolutionised watch production without sacrificing the quality for which they were now famous. In the 1900s the factory began producing the newly developed wristwatches, receiving orders from the American forces. In the 1920s the company made its first *Grande*

Four watches by Vacheron Constantin. Left top: a chronograph. Bottom left: a chronometer. Middle: a gold square watch with stepped case. Right: a rare gold rectangular wristwatch with raised curved glass. Only 30 pieces were made in the early 1950s.

complication, a minute repeater with split-seconds chronograph, perpetual calendar, moon phase and alarm, but it really concentrated on high-quality timepieces for normal use. The present line contains about 100 models spread over five major collections: 'Phideas' (the flagship line), 'Les Historiques' (reflecting the traditional design of the past), 'Les Absolues' (which pays homage to the jeweller's art), 'Les Complications' (displaying all the technical skills of the master watchmaker) and 'Les Essentials' (a collection of round, gold-cased watches on a strap). Vacheron Constantin is

one of the few remaining manufacturers which makes all its own movements and parts and assemble them in its own factories.

BREGUET

Another of the great houses, Breguet now comprises three companies: Montres Breguet, watchmakers since 1775; Nouvelle Lamania, a movement manufacturer; and Valdar, a specialist in microelectrical engineering. The founder of the company, Abraham-Louis Breguet, is acknowledged as the greatest watchmaker of all time, and is credited with

either inventing or patenting the majority of horological achievements, including, in 1780, the perpetual or automatic movement, the development of the perpetual-date calendar, the Breguet balance spring, the tourbillon, the parachut shock-absorber, the double-barrelled marine chronometer, and perhaps the first wristwatch, made for the Queen of Naples in 1810. During the Battle of Waterloo, Wellington and Napoleon both consulted their Breguet watches. Breguet today specialises in mechanical watches of considerable technical workmanship in finely wrought cases, and has three product lines: 'Classic', ultra-thin hand-wound or self-winding chronographs or tourbillons; 'Marine', automatic and water-resistant; and 'Type XX Aeronavale', a re-issue of a 1950s' model developed for the French naval air service. An automatic chronograph, it has all the features of the original: black dial, tritium-coated hands and numerals, rotating bezel and the famous *retour au vol* function, which returns the chronograph to zero and immediately restarts it.

Above: The 1928 Vacheron Constantin Grand complication pocket watch in 18-carat gold with perpetual calendar, moon phases in lapis lapuli, minute repeater with chimes, alarm and split-second chronograph movement.

Right: The flagship line of Breguet, the 'Marine' series, here in 18-carat white gold, with the bezel and bracelet links studded with diamonds.

CHAUMET

Established in Paris in 1780, Chaumet has a long tradition of creating fine jewellery for the courts of Europe since the time of Emperor Napoleon I, when the firm's founder, Marie-Etienne Nitot, was appointed court jeweller in 1804. Nitot, as well as creating fabulous pieces of jewellery, also made watches set with precious stones, which were often given as mementos to diplomats and friends of the court. Now part of the international group Investcorps, which also has interests in Nouvelle Lamania and Gucci, Chaumet's collection includes the 'Anneau' line of watches with quartz movements in silver or gold round cases, and a series of interchangeable bracelets

in alligator skin, lambs skin, pearls, satin or gold, and, if desired, with diamonds. 'Les Pleiades' is a 'jumping-hour' model: the polished case features two windows, one displays the hours, the other the minutes. The hour, as the name implies, jumps forward every 60 minutes. 'Aquila II' is a masculine-size line of quartz watches with day/date, while the flagship line is the 'Khesis' collection for women, all of which have square cases with a curved profile. The collection takes its name from the Navajo for the sun, the emblem of the Place Vendôme in Paris, home of Chaumet.

Top: Design for a watch for the Duchesse de Luynes.

Bottom: Watches from Chaumet's 'Khesis' collection. Shown here are the 'Classic Lady' and 'Top Lady' models.

GIRARD PERREGAUX

Girard Perregaux can trace its beginnings back to Geneva in 1791, when Jean François Bautte, who had started work at the age of 12, at 19 created two beautiful watches which caused his employer Jacques Dauphin to make him a partner. By 1830 the firm was employing 300 workers, and its products – movements, cases, dials and jewelled watches – were well known and highly regarded. In 1897 the firm received an order from the German navy for 2,000 of the new wristwatches – the world's first mass-produced ones – which were a great success, though when it tried to export them to the United States, they were not well received. After World War II, the firm, known for its technical research, patented the 'Gyromatic' (1957), a device which allows for very flat automatics, and produced movements with increasingly high frequency – up to 36,000 vph. Girard Perregaux was one of the first of the great houses to venture into electronics, producing its own quartz movements in 1969 and, in 1970, launching its first quartz watch. Nevertheless, the company's heart was in the creation of complicated mechanical masterpieces such as the tourbillon with three golden bridges in 1982. Each watch took eight months to complete; the limited edition of 20 watches was finally finished in 1990, and the following year it was decided that a wristwatch version should be made. The limited series is now a highly prized collector's item, but the flagship line is a tribute to the race-car manufacturers Ferrari. Launched in 1993, the collection started with a split-second chronograph in 18-carat white gold mounted on a strap. Later models include, among others, a stainless-steel automatic chronograph with flyback hand and date.

JAEGER-LECOULTRE

Jaeger-LeCoultre still occupies the same site in the village of Le Sentier in the Vallee de Joux where it was established in 1833 by Charles Antoine LeCoultre. The Jaeger name comes from the company's merger nearly a century later with the watch division of a French marine-chronometer-maker, Edward Jaeger, who, having worked with the firm for 20 years, was taken into partnership. By the end of the 19th century, the company specialised in chronographs, minute repeaters and alarm watches, and in 1903 it was making the world's thinnest watch movements in regular production. It was in 1931 that Jaeger-LeCoultre produced the watch that brought them international fame – the 'Reverso', where the rectangular case flipped over and turned its back on the world to protect the delicate movement. This design, it is said, was in response to demands from British officers in India for a watch that could withstand the rigours of a polo match! The 'Reverso' is still the company's flagship line, and has included the 'Reverso Tourbillon', the 60th Jubilee model (1991); the 'Reverso Chronograph Retrograde'; the 'Reverso Joaillerie' (bedecked with diamonds); and the 'Reverso 101', with the world's smallest mechanical movement.

Above: Girard Perregaux's 'Ferrari' chronograph with flyback hand. A limited-edition watch launched in tribute to Ferrari.

Right: The prize-winning tourbillon with three golden bridges from Girard Perregaux.

BAUME ET MERCIER

In 1542, while watchmaking was still in its infancy, the Baume family set up a workshop in Les Bois in the Swiss Jura. In 1834, its descendants registered the Société Baume Frères as manufacturers of complete watches. In 1918 William Baume joined with Paul Mercier, and the firm of Baume et Mercier was born. The fortunes of the firm were consistent, if undistinguished, and in the mid-1950s the firm of Piaget took over. Baume et Mercier was now

Right: A magnificent variation on the 'Reverso' theme is this 'Joaillerie' version, with the case and bracelet encrusted with diamonds.

in a position to market an extremely flat automatic, but by then the electronic age had arrived, and in 1971 it produced one of the first tuning-fork watches. From then on quartz technology was to play an increasing part in its production, and the last of its own mechanical movements was made in 1983. In 1988 both Baume et Mercier and its holding company, Piaget, were acquired by Cartier International, and among its current lines are the 'Hampton', with a somewhat Art-Deco-styled case; the 'Malibu' sports watch; 'Linea' (ladies' fashion watches); and the 18-carat-gold watches that epitomise Baume et Mercier's traditional production, the 'Classic' collection. The flagship line, conceived in 1973, is the 'Riviera series', with its unique, 12-sided case.

Right: The flagship line of Jaeger-LeCoultre remains the 'Reverso' in all its forms, including this, the chronograph version.

Far right: The 'Hampton' from Baume et Mercier, with its distinctive, curved steel case.

PATEK PHILIPPE

One of the most prestigious Swiss watch brands of all time, the firm had its unlikely beginning in a meeting between a former Polish cavalry officer and an inventive French watchmaker. Antoine de Pradwicz, fleeing his country after a failed coup against the Russian Tsar Nicholas I, ended up in Geneva and changed his name to Patek. In 1844 he met Adrien Philippe and between them they produced a number of innovative models, including the first to have independent second hands and a 'free' main spring. Their aim was to produce the best watches in the world and their output matched their ambition. Over the next few years they won more than 500 international awards, and produced perhaps the world's first wristwatch in 1868 – although it was to be another 50 years before a commercially viable version was made. Other of the firm's inventions include the double chronograph with sweep seconds, a perpetual-calendar mechanism and an improved regulator. In the 20th century it remained at the forefront of horological developments: by 1952 it had a battery-operated solid-state clock, and in 1962 it developed the master-clock system still in use for time-keeping in Switzerland's airports and public buildings. Today, 80 per cent of Patek's ladies' watches and 20 per cent of

Above: The building in Geneva, the headquarters of Patek Philippe since the firm was founded in 1844.

Below: 'Malibu' from Baume et Mercier – the perfect balance between the classic and the sports watch.

Below: Five Patek Phillipe watches – the watch second from the right is a Rolex.

mens' models have slim quartz movements, and the most popular designs remain those watches in the 'Calatrava' collection, first launched in 1932.

CARTIER

The name of Cartier has been synonymous with luxury goods since Louis-François Cartier took over the workshop of the master jeweller Adolphe Picard in Paris in 1847. Cartier was a jeweller first and a watchmaker second, and his dazzling creations were bought by the rich and famous in the courts of Europe for their beauty – their time-keeping was secondary. In 1904, a friend, Alberto Santos-Dumont, asked him to make an accurate timepiece to check the performance of his airship. Louis Cartier got together with a Swiss colleague, Edward Jaeger, to design one especially for him; it was Cartier's first wrist-watch and it opened up a new chapter in the firm's history. Cartier introduced the 'Tonneau' model (named after the type of barrel in which the French store wine) and in 1917 the 'Tank', which remains Cartier's most memorable design and includes 11 different versions. In 1996 Cartier launched the 'Tank Française', a square model with a slightly curved gold case and integrated bracelet, and black Roman numerals and winder with sapphire cabochon.

Above left: The small 18-carat mechanical Cartier 'Tonneau'.

Left: Cartier's 18-carat automatic 'Santos'.

OMEGA

When, in 1969, Neil Armstrong made his first 'giant leap for mankind', he also gave a hefty boost to one of Switzerland's best-known watch brands. Armstrong's watch was a hand-wound mechanical chronograph, and one that by today's standards was pretty convention-al. Founded in 1848 by Louis Brandt, by the end of the century his organisation had be-come one of the largest factories in Switzerland, producing around 100,000 watch-es a year, and the name Omega appeared for the first time. In addition to being appointed official time-keeper to 21 Olympic Games, Omega watches were worn by Virgil Grissom in the *Gemini 3* space mission in 1965 and by the Russian *Soyuz* crew in 1975. The compa-ny has developed both quartz and mechani-cal models in a vast range for men and women, from classical dress watches and gem-set cre-ations to complicated chronographs and chronometers for specialist purposes. The 'Constellation' is its flagship line and heir to the long tradition of precision records.

TISSOT

Tissot is the leading name in SMH's (Société Suisse de Microeletronique et d'Horlorgerie) mid-priced watches , accounting for over half the sales in this sector, the others being Pierre Balmain, Hamilton, Certina and Mido. Tissot had its origins in 1853, when Charles-Emile Tissot returned to Le Locle after working in America for five years and persuaded his fa-ther to open a watch factory. Their watches were sold to dealers in the USA and then to Russia, a market which the Tissots particu-larly cultivated and which became their biggest customer up to the revolution in 1917. In 1904 the imperial court had given Tissot an order for a pocket watch to be awarded to

officers for special services, and the first wrist-watch was produced in 1915. In 1930 the com-pany broke new ground with the production of the first anti-magnetic watch, and the Tissot 'Navigator' was the first automatic watch with an international calendar which could display world time as well as local time. Tissot ush-ered in the electronic age by developing a new magnetic clutch which facilitated accurate au-tomatic time-zone changes, while in 1985 it launched the first 'Rock Watch', in which the case was made of Swiss granite millions of years old. In 1991 they added the ceramic 'Creation' watch to the collection, and many of Tissot's unique watches have become col-lector's items.

Above: The 'Tank', Cartier's most memo-rable – and desirable – design, comes in 11 different versions.

Below: Heir to the long tradition of preci-sion records, the 'Constellation' is Omega's flagship line.

Above: The flagship line, 'Calatrava', from Patek Philippe, with its unusal hands and pyramidal hour markers.

CHOPARD

In 1860 Louis-Ulysse Chopard set up a small factory in Sonviller in the Swiss Jura to make pocket watches – which were particularly favoured by railway employees for their reliability. Later, his son branched out into jewellery watches, and the distinctive blend of high fashion and fine watchmaking became the hallmark of Chopard in more than 50 countries. The flagship of their horological jewellery is their 'Happy Diamonds' concept, in which seven diamonds edged with gold float freely around the dial between two plates of scratch-proof sapphire crystal.

TAG-HEUER

Since its inception, TAG-Heuer has been associated with sporting events, a reputation consistent with the aims of its 20-year-old founder Edward Heuer, who began making chronographs for sportsmen as far back as 1860. The list of Heuer's achievements is impressive: the first timer with 1/10th second-measuring capability (1916); official time-keeper to the Olympics in Antwerp (1912), Paris (1924) and Amsterdam (1928); inventor of a flyback mechanism (1930); and launcher of an automotive instrument with interchangeable dials (1933). In 1974 Heuer was appointed official time-keeper to the Ferrari Formula 1 racing team, and in 1980 it was official time keeper to its last Olympic Games, in Moscow. In 1985 Heuer was taken over by TAG (Techniques d'Avant Garde), a French company specialising in advanced technologies, and the company became TAG-Heuer. Its top-of-the-line

Right: Seven diamonds for good luck float freely above the dial in Chopard's 'Happy Diamonds' line.

collection includes the '6000' series, but the 1964 'Heuer Carrera', the first Heuer watch to bear a name, remains equally desirable.

a chronograph with chronometer performance using the El Primero movement first launched at the 1969 Basle Fair.

Above left: The top-of-the-line TAG-Heuer '6000' series, the '6000 Gold Automatic'.

Above: The 1964 'Heuer Carrera'.

ZENITH

From its very beginnings, Zenith was different to the conventional watch-producing house: its founder, Georges Favre-Jacot, in 1865 decided to go straight into the production of complete watches, using up-to-date machinery and tools which he designed and made himself. Now producing high-quality watches – both mechanical and quartz – the 'Class 6' automatic watch with the Elite movement is the star performer in Zenith's collection, rivalled only by the popular 'ChronoMaster',

LONGINES

In 1832 Auguste Aggassiz set up his business in St Imer in the Jura mountains. It was a trading house and consisted of a purchasing office which bought in watch parts which were then assembled by home-workers; a workshop where the finished watches were finished and adjusted; and a sales office consisting of Aggassiz himself, who, having organised all the work, took to the road to sell the finished products. When Charles Lindbergh made the world's first solo crossing of the Atlantic in

Above: The sturdy, yet elegant, Longines quartz 'Lindbergh' watch.

his monoplane, *The Spirit of St Louis*, he navigated by means of his Longines wristwatch. During the 33-hour flight, Lindbergh kept himself awake by designing a watch to help pilots establish their longitude, and his sketch was the basis for Longines' 'Lindbergh-hour Angle' watch, which appeared in 1937 and was an instant success. Perhaps to overcome the somewhat staid appearance of its main collection, Longines launched its 'Golden Wings' line, named after the famous winged-hourglass trademark, and aimed at the younger market, while the 'Conquest VHP', launched in 1984, has been Longines' most successful line.

IWC: THE INTERNATIONAL WATCH CO

In the 1860s an American who was to make a lasting impression on the Swiss watch scene visited Switzerland with the idea of setting up a watch factory to take advantage of lower wages and local expertise. In 1869, Florentine Ariosto Jones from Boston settled in Schaffhausen in eastern Switzerland, where he was offered a factory with hydroelectric power from the Rhine. Jones, who had visions of exporting his products back to the USA, called his company the International Watch Co and since its early days it has made watchmaking history. Jones' original, 18-ligne calibres, among the first watches to feature crown winding, are collector's treasures, while to mark the company's 125th anniversary, the 'Destriero Scafusa' was built in a series of just 125 watches which retailed in Britain at £125,000 each. The flagship line is the 'Mark XII Pilot's' watch, driven by two quartz movements and double-stepping motors.

PIAGET

Many Swiss watchmaking companies go back a long way, but it is rare to find one still

Above: A contemporary classic from Longines' 'Conquest' line.

in the hands of a member of the original family. Although Piaget, founded by Georges Piaget in 1874, became part of the Richemont Group in 1988, the day-to-day control remained in the hands of Yves Piaget, great-grandson of the founder. Since the 1960s Piaget has been renowned for its 'Haute Joaillerie' watches, and its ultra-thin movements allowed it to pioneer the use of hard stones such as lapis lazuli, coral, mother-of-pearl, and tiger-eye in an unusual and exciting range of dials. Since many of its watches are very limited editions, Piaget says that it has no flagship line, but the 'Citea' model is probably the nearest to a 'popular' line.

AUDEMARS PIGUET

Jules Audemar and Edward Piguet were 24 and 22 years old respectively when they established the Audemars Piguet manufactory in 1875 with the aim of creating the finest watches in the world. From the beginning the firm specialised in complex watches: it produced its first *Grande complication*, a gold hunter, in 1889. The year 1906 saw its first wristwatch with a minute repeater, and in 1920 it introduced the world's smallest minute repeater and, five years later, the world's thinnest pocket watch. In 1972 Audemars Piguet launched its flagship line of mechanical watches in steel cases, with hexagonal screws fastening the bezel, called 'Royal Oak' in honour of the British Royal Navy's ships of that line bearing the name.

SEIKO

It is tempting to think of Seiko, one of Japan's leading watch and clock manufacturers, as a phenomenon of the high-tech revolution, but in fact the company has a pedigree as long as many of its Swiss contemporaries, for it was

founded in Tokyo when the jeweller named Kitaro Hattori formed Hattori and Co, and then the next year a second company, Seikosha, to meet the growing demand for clocks which followed Japan's adoption of the 24-hour time zone. In 1895 Hattori began to produce pocket watches and, in 1918, wristwatch production began. By 1936 theit was responsible for 60 per cent of Japan's horological output.

Above: Piaget claims not to have a flagship line, since many of its watches are limited editions. The 'Citea' model is probably the nearest thing to a 'popular' line.

Today, Seiko's flagship is the 'Kinetic' line of battery-operated quartz models that run on electricity that is generated by the wearer's own body movements.

BREITLING

In 1884 Louis Breitling opened a studio workshop in La Chaux de Fonds, realising that the new inventions of the internal-combustion engine by Gottfried Daimler and the gasoline-driven automobile produced by Karl Benz would lead to great things, and that they would need timing instruments. In 1936 the firm devised a cockpit chronograph for planes and, in 1952, the watch that became its international trademark, the 'Navitimer', the favourite of pilots across the world. Ten years later, the 'Cosmonaute', the supersonic version, appeared. The best-selling 'Chronomat' was originally designed for the RAF's Red Arrows, but the most ingenious is the 'Emergency', a wrist-worn instrument for pilots that, in addition to chronomatic functions, incorporates a tiny transistor which, in the event of an accident, can transmit a signal on the international distress frequency to assist rescuers.

INGERSOLL

Robert Ingersoll staked his claim to a place in horological history when, in 1892, he launched his 'Dollar' watch, a watch a working man could buy with a day's pay. He called it the 'Yankee', gave away a chain and advertised it as the 'Watch that made the dollar famous'. Another success was his wristwatch for soldiers in World War I, adapted from a lady's pocket watch and sold with a protective grid over the dial. Other models had luminous hands and numbers; by 1918 more than 85 per cent of Ingersoll watches had the new 'Radiolite' dials, as they were named. Famous

wearers of Ingersoll watches have included the writer Mark Twain, the aviator Sir Alan Cobham and the inventor Thomas Edison. Ingersoll's current output consists of some 100 models, but its flagship line must surely be the 'Nurse Fob', first introduced in the early 1950s, which remains largely unchanged, but ever popular.

Above: The 'Nurse Fob' from Ingersoll, originally introduced in the 1950s.

Above: This 'Old Navitimer' is a good example of Breitling's craftsmanship.

20TH-CENTURY WATCHMAKERS

Of the estimated 653 million watches manufactured in 1988 (according to the survey carried out by Citizen), 123 million were mechanical, 228 million were digital and 308 million were analogue watches. The biggest maker of wristwatches was Japan (260 million), followed by Hong Kong (170 million, all digital) and Switzerland (75 million). As with many other industries in the 20th century, Japan's export achievements dominate, but it is interesting to note that, conversely, Swiss watches increased their share of the Japanese market from 18 to 20 per cent in 1988.

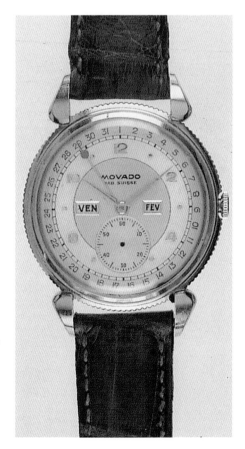

Right: A gold day/date watch by Movado, bearing the words 'Fab. Suisse' ('Swiss made') – the guarantee of a fine watch.

Previous page: A superb collection of wristwatches auctioned at Sotheby's in London in 1987.

Brand-marketing today is as important as it was 50 years ago, but the difference today is that very few of the 'names' manufacture every part of a wristwatch. There are 'assemblers' at the bottom end of the market; the 'own-brand' market continues to expand rapidly, with Endura one of the leaders in this field. When the invasion of quartz-powered movements overtook Switzerland at the beginning of the 1970s, many manufacturers disposed of their machinery for making mechanical watches. Oris, among others, was fortunate in retaining its plant, and is thus well positioned to re-enter the market for mechanicals – a market which has never really vanished. At the time of the quartz invasion, many great watch names disappeared; many more were forced to sell out to larger groups. Today, in Switzerland, SMH owns the companies Certina, Endura, Hamilton, Longines, Mido, Rado, Swatch and Tissot. In Japan, the family-controlled Hattori owns the firms Jean Lassale, Lorus, Pulsar, Seiko and Yema.

The words 'Swiss made' still remain a guarantee of a fine wristwatch, and the watchmaking centres continue in the Swiss cities, towns and villages of Bienne, Geneva, Grenchen, La Chaux de Fonds, Le Brassus, Le Locle, Le Sentier, Lausanne, Neufchatel,

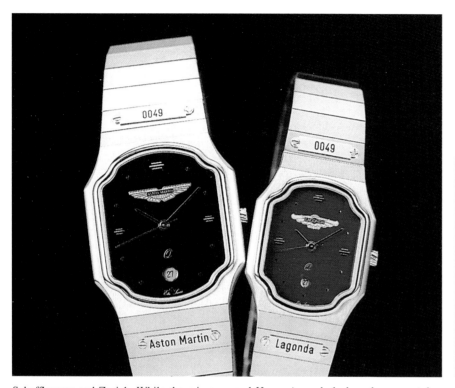

Left: Aston Martin Lagonda recently commissioned a limited number of wristwatches, each for its two classic-cars marques. Each watch was serially numbered.

Above: The 1996 limited-edition mechanical alarm by Oris, a unique and highly collectable watch.

Schaffhausen and Zurich. While there is no longer a watchmaking industry of any size in America or the UK, Pforzheim in Germany remains a traditional manufacturing centre.

THE FUTURE OF WRISTWATCHES

The future of the wristwatch is assured, as annual sales now exceed 800 million a year; each of us can now own several watches for different occasions (business, evening, sports, casual weekends) and the market for children's watches is growing; novelty watches encourage collecting habits. The market for expensive mechanical analogues is also increasing, and great automobile marques and fashion houses (Ferrari, Yves Saint Laurent, Gucci, and Hermes) regularly launch new watches as line extensions.

ORIS

The first 20th-century manufacturer of watches, Oris, founded in 1904 by Paul Cattin and Georges Christian, has always been a company with more than a hint of independence. In 1938 Oris began making complete watches and produced the 'Pointer Calendar' model which has remained a feature of the Oris collection ever since. A Swiss law enacted in the 1930s regulating the production of watches effectively prohibited Oris from producing jewelled-lever watches, as well as certain forms of shock-resistant systems allied to jewelled

levers. To demonstrate that the watches it produced were accurate and properly made, it entered some of the models in official timing trials, and to its delight was awarded official certification which allowed it to call its watches 'chronometers'. Today Oris makes only jewelled-lever mechanical watches, and over the years has produced many innovations: automatics with reserve-power displays (1952), its first chronograph (1970), its first mechanical alarm (produced in limited series in 1988). Its flagship line is undoubtedly the 'Big Crown'; originally designed for the US Air Force during World War II, it meant easy operation when wearing gloves.

ROLEX

One of the best-known names in watches, the story of Rolex begins in 1905, when Hans Wilsdorf set up his own company in England, and by 1910 he was awarded the first-ever official chronometer certificate for a wristwatch. At the end of World War I the company transferred operations to Geneva and was re-named Montres Rolex SA, and the task was now to design a truly waterproof case. By 1926 there was a prototype, and samples were tested under water for three weeks: the Rolex 'Oyster' had arrived. When cross-Channel swimmer Mercedes Gleitz stepped ashore at Dover, Wilsdorf made sure that photographers were on hand to see that the Rolex was still working properly! For 50 years, the 'Oyster' has remained largely the same, while the company continued at the cutting edge of watch design. The 'Datejust', launched in 1945, was the first chronometer with automatic date

Above: The Oris 'Big Crown' chronometer, designed for easy operation when wearing gloves.

Right: Rolex's front-page advertisement for its 'Oyster' wristwatch, 24 November 1927 and the real thing: one of the most famous of all collectable watches.

change; the 1950s saw the 'Submariner', the first wristwatch as guaranteed water-resistant at 330 feet (91.5m); and in 1971 the 'Sea Dweller' for divers was launched, complete with helium valve to cope with decompression. Meanwhile, on top of the world, Edmund Hilary took a Rolex 'Explorer' to more than 29,000 feet (8,839m) when he scaled Everest in 1953. While there are the 'Cellini' collection and the 'Tudor' collections, Rolex's flagship remains the 'Oyster Perpetual Datejust',

Above: The rectangular Rolex 'Prince' (left) and the chic, plain and simple Rolex 'Oyster Perpetual' (right).

Left: Pages from an early Rolex Watch Co Ltd brochure promoting an early Rolex 'Oyster', c.1934.

the most popular model being the 'President'.

EBEL

The 'Fabrique Ebel, Blum et Cie' was founded in 1911 by Eugene Blum, who made up the company name by combining his initials with his wife Alice's family name – Eugene Blum et Levy – EBEL – and the brand name first came to prominence in 1914 by winning a gold medal at the Swiss National Exhibition. Until the 1970s Ebel was known for its fairly conventional, if technically sound, watches. The 'Sports' collection and the 'Beluga' line had been successful, but in 1970 the firm acquired and restored a villa designed by the Modernist architect Le Corbusier and, inspired by these surroundings, the company launched the 'Architects of Time' collection, which has remained its theme ever since.

FORTIS

Fortis was launched in 1912 in Grenchen by Walter Vogt, who began by making gold-cased mechanical watches. In 1926 Vogt met John Harwood who, two years earlier, had invented the self-winding wristwatch, and at the Basle Trade Fair that year, Fortis launched the world's first automatic watch in serial production (there had been small limited series previously.) Fortis went on to build a reputation for sturdy, accurate watches, but a benchmark was the introduction in 1968 of the 'Flipper', a colourful line of fun watches with water-resistant cases. Pre-Swatch, it was one of the pioneers

Top: The 'Beluga' line from Ebel: 'Round', 'Tonneau' and 'Carree', made only of gold and available in a single size.

Right: The Ebel gold '1911' watch, with heavy, gold integrated bracelet.

Belos left: The 'Fortis Harwood', named after the inventor of the world's first automatic wristwatch.

Below centre: The flagship line of Fortis: the limited-edition 'Cosmonaut's Chronograph' watch.

Below right: Rado's 'DiaStar Ceramica'. Bracelet, case and crown are in scratchproof, high-tech ceramic, with four diamonds on the dial.

of the pop-watch era. In 1996, to mark the 35th anniversary of manned space flights (Fortis has been part of the official equipment of the European-Russian space mission since 1994), Fortis produced an 18-carat-gold version of 'Cosmonaut's Chronograph', first developed in association with the Yuri Gagarin Cosmonauts Training Centre.

RADO

In 1917, the brothers Fritz, Ernst and Werner Schlup started production of watch movements in Lengnau, and sold their products to

American importers, a connection that would last for the next 30 years, when they started to make complete watches for other firms. The most popular design of the early period was the 'Starliner', a robust watch with water-resistance to 12 atmospheres, thanks to a system exclusive to Rado. Many of the watches it sold had gold cases which frequently got scratched and needed repolishing. The company set out to find a scratchproof material, and developed a compound of titanium carbide and tungsten before launching its first case in 1962, calling the watch the 'DiaStar',

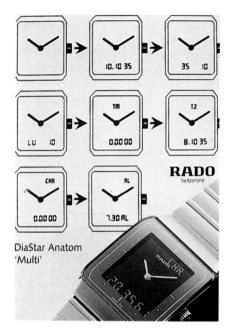

DiaStar Anatom
'Multi'

Above: The 'DiaStar Multi,' one of Rado's most popular lines.

Right: Michel Herbelin's flagship line, the 'Newport', introduced in 1995, in rectangular cases with rounded corners.

which was a sensation in both design and construction. Since that launch, Rado has continued to build its reputation for scratchproof and innovative design. The 'Ceramic', launched in 1989, had the bracelet as well as the case and crown made from high-tech materials, and its latest innovation is the 'Anatom Multi', a square-cased model with seven functions, all on command at the turn of the crown.

CITIZEN

Citizen, the world's largest watchmaker, with around 21 per cent of global production, was founded in 1930 in Japan, and, in its brief history, has produced a significant number of top technical watches. With Citizen, sci-fi and James Bond-type gizmos and gadgets become facts of life! Among its highlights are the world's flattest watch, the world's smallest quartz movement and a professional diver's watch, the Citizen 'Hyper Aqualand', which is capable of communicating with a PC. The 'Space Master Chronograph' – the world's first radio-controlled watch with chronograph functions in analogue display – is a supreme example of Citizen's innovative technology. This watch sets itself once a day, switches automatically from summer to winter time, has self-illuminating numbers and hands, a stopwatch accurate to 1/20th second, a tachometer and also an alarm. The high-tech antenna is incorporated invisibly into the casing.

MICHEL HERBELIN

In 1946 Michel Herbelin opened his workshop on the French side of the Jura mountains, just across the border from Switzerland. To start with, he assembled private-label watches for other companies, concentrating on quality manufacture. Aspiring to have his own line, in 1968 he launched his first collection under

Above: Citizen's 'Eco-Drive', with radio control.

Above: The Timex 'Datalink' and 'Datalink with Indiglo', which can be linked to personal computers, and the Timex 'Timberland'.

his own name. The line is noted for the softness of the contours, harmonious dimensions and subtle details. The current collection contains three main lines: the 'Classics' line, the 'Sports' line – epitomised by 'Newport', the flagship collection – and 'Safari'. The lines include chronographs, as well as normal timekeepers. The 'Newport' line, especially the rectangular cases with rounded corners introduced in 1995, have Swiss quartz movements, sapphire crystals and screw-down crowns, and are water-resistant to 165 feet (50m).

TIMEX

Founded in the United States in 1950, Timex is perhaps best known as a multi-brand organisation which markets more than 200 different models under its corporate umbrella. Split over 15 different names, such as 'Wizards', 'Star Trek' and 'Essentials', all fall within a reasonable price bracket. Timex is one of the world's leading watch manufacturers, and has an impressive share of the important children's market. Furthermore, it is also prominent in licensing deals – with the Disney organisation, the Guess? group, and recently with American footwear and sports-clothing company, Timberland. One of its most popular normal models is the 'Mercury', a watch originally launched in 1959 and relaunched in 1995 with the addition of Indiglo night light, while its current outstanding technical innovation is the 'Datalink', which works with Microsoft Office for Windows 95!

CORUM

Founded by Gaston Reis in partnership with his nephew Rene Bannwart in 1955, Corum soon developed a reputation not only for the high quality of its watches, but also for the originality of its designs. Examples include

Above: The Corum 'Golden Bridge'. The 18-carat-gold mechanism is suspended like a golden bridge in a clear sapphire crystal.

Above: Corum's 'Admiral's Cup', which many regard as the classic watch for the future. Enamelled nautical pennants mark the hours and, naturally, it is waterproof.

the 'Golden Tube', the 'Chinese Hat' and the 'Longchamp' (with its concealed lugs), which are all now collector's pieces. An outstanding technical innovation is the 'Golden Bridge', in which the tiny 18-carat-gold parts of the movement, with its straight-line geartrain, are suspended in clear sapphire crystal. But Corum's most famous collection is the 'Admiral's Cup', a 12-sided case corresponding to the hours, with pennants indicating the numbers 1 to 12 in the International Maritime Code. The company no longer makes all its own movements, but selects the best examples from other houses – Piaget and Jaeger-LeCoultre – but all Corum watches, whether quartz or mechanical, are hand-finished in-house by its own craftsmen.

GERALD GENTA

While it gives the impression of being a one-man band, the company, founded in 1969, in fact has two centres of production: Geneva and Le Brassus, and employs some 120 people. Genta himself conceives the designs for each new watch, and his drawings are passed to his team which, with the aid of micromechanical processors and computer technology, turn out the gears, pinions and other parts which are meticulously hand-finished, that go into a Gerald Genta watch. Sometimes this process can take months, even years, before the piece is ready to leave the workroom. The 'Fantasies' collection applied this degree of skill and care to Mickey Mouse, Minnie Mouse and Donald Duck, on mother-of-pearl dials and 18-carat-gold cases! But the flagship is surely the appropriately named 'Success'. A new concept in case design, in the treatment of the dial and crystal, the watch can be hand-wound or automatic, quartz or mechanical or have a chronograph movement.

Above: Gerald Genta's 'Fantasies' watch, with Minnie Mouse pointing out the hours.

MAURICE LACROIX

Maurice Lacroix was founded in 1975 in Sainelegier in the Jura, but in that short time it has acquired an outstanding reputation. In fact, it is said to be the second-largest-selling Swiss watch in Germany after Rolex. Part of the Desco Group, which distributes Swiss watch brands throughout the Far and Middle East, the movements of Lacroix watches range from ETA quartz to mechanical *complications*. The current line contains about 100 models, divided into a number of collections: 'Fabia', 'Calypso' and 'Les Mechaniques', with the top of the range 'Masterpiece Collection' with its jumping-hour model. The recently released 'Venus Chronograph', in a solid-platinum case housing a complicated, hand-decorated chronograph movement, was produced in a limited collector's edition of just 125 pieces.

RAYMOND WEIL

Founded in 1976, Raymond Weil is one of the few brands of watches to bear the name of the man who actually makes them (individual creative horologists apart). With global sales of more than half a million pieces a year, Raymond Weil has become a major producer among Swiss watch houses, and can claim to rank at fourth place in the hierarchy. There are eight collections in Raymond Weil's total output, many of them named after pieces of classical music or opera; the main brand is 'Parsifal', with approximately 50 different designs and accounting for 35 per cent of worldwide sales, followed by 'Fidelio', 'Tango' and 'Toccata'. Two of its earlier models were the 'Golden Eagle', with a distinctive, octagonal case and gold studs on the bezel, and 'Traviata', a gold integrated-bracelet watch for men and women, with unusual dials like stained-glass windows.

Above: Gerald Genta's flagship line, with a totally new concept in case deisgn, appropriately called 'Success'.

Above: The 'Calypso', inspired by the Calypso, a ship owned by the French underwater explorer Jacques Cousteau.

Above: Raymond Weil watches from the 'Traviata' collection.

SWISS ARMY WATCHES

This brand was launched in 1978 by the Forschner Group (which originated in New Britain, Connecticut in 1855, selling butcher's knives), which is also the distributor of the Victorinox Swiss Army knife. All the qualities of the knife – durability, dependability, fitness for purpose, together with Swiss engineering and value for money – were the very virtues that would help sell a similar product, namely, a Swiss watch. Initially the line consisted of just three models in two sizes. Its features were rugged designs, uncluttered lines and easy-to-read dials, all driven by a reliable Swiss quartz movement. The first line was called the 'Original', and is still the best-selling line in the collection, which has been extended to 30 different models, closely followed by the 'Officers' line.

HUBLOT

In Geneva in 1980, Carlo Crocco founded the firm whose name in French means 'porthole', and the simple round case of Hublot watches, with tiny titanium screws on the bezel at the numerical points, is very reminiscent of a ship's window on the world. The classical design is combined with a water-protected case in precious metal and a rubber strap. This is no ordinary rubber band, however: it took three years to research and develop its supple resilience and sensuous satin finish with steel fastening inserts at bezel and clasp. The unusual straps are made exclusively for Hublot in Italy, and are the only part of the watch therefore that cannot be said to be Swiss made.

Left: 'Officers', from Swiss Army Watches, come in two sizes and offer a choice of polished, black or red bezel on a leather strap.

The company's latest creations have dials in vibrant colours, toned down by fine honeycomb texturing. With quartz movements and sapphire crystal, they are water-resistant to 165 feet (50m).

CHRONOSWISS

Against the then prevailing trend for quartz movements in watches, in 1983 Gerd R Lang, a German watchmaker, set out to manufacture mechanical wristwatches only. Lang was convinced that there was a market among collectors and connoisseurs for limited editions of high-quality watches based on well-known Swiss calibres and hand-finished to precise standards in his own workshops. While the designs were traditional, the production made use of the latest in technology. Although based in Munich, the company was named Chronoswiss because Lang intended to have only the finest Swiss movements. Lang's first watch was produced in 1982: a chronograph with moon phase and date, and limited in number. All are now collector's pieces or in museums. Today there are several lines in the collection: 'Kairos', 'Klassik' and 'Cabrio', which, at the touch of a button at six o'clock, flips over the centre of the watch to reveal the back of the decorated movement, protected by scratchproof sapphire crystal. 'Orea' models have genuine enamel dials – something of a rarity, even among better watches, but since production is so small and each model is made in very limited quantities, there is no flagship line – just remarkable, beautiful and desirable watches.

Hublot's Green/Blue Dials, the company's latest creation.

Left: The 'Kairos' chronograph, from Chronoswiss. Each of the company's models is made in very limited quantities.

Far left: The Chronoswiss 'Orea', with hand-made, baked-enamel dial, blue-steel hands and scratchproof sapphire crystal.

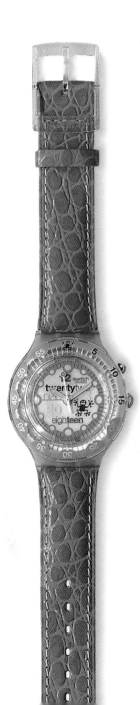

SWATCH

The Swatch story begins in 1978, when Switzerland's watch industry was under great pressure from Japan. The inexpensive watch market, which Swiss pin-lever watches had previously dominated, had been virtually lost to the new quartz models from the Far East. Dr Ernst Thomke, then head of ETA, the movement division of SMH, challenged his technicians to beat the Japanese: he wanted a slimmer, better quartz movement. Six months later, the prototype, at a mere 2mm high and the thinnest in the world, was produced, and one of the features of the watch was that it used the back of the case as the backplate. It was launched as the 'Concord Delirium'. A quartz watch produced semi-automatically, its components were reduced from 91 to just 51 parts in a plastic, waterproof case – shock-resistant, durable, affordable and immensely popular. The Swatch was born. By 1985, 10 million had been made. 'Pop' Swatch and 'Maxi' Swatch were introduce, and in 1987 the first Christmas special. The year 1989 saw the first Swatch Telecom product, the 'Twinphone', and by now 50 million Swatches had been sold; the 'Puff' specials in a pristine set of six sold for $120,000! By 1992 the Swatch Collector's Club had been formed, and numerous other Swatch 'gadgets' had appeared: Swatch automatics, chronographs and the Swatch pager with integrated radio receiver. Around 150 different designs are introduced each year in four seasonal collections, and in 1996 Swatch was appointed official time-keeper to the Atlanta Olympic Games – an event marked, of course, by a special-edition Swatch in two versions: gold for athletes, silver for fans. All designs, whatever their cost, are in limited editions of up to 30,000 pieces. None are repeated or carried over. Swatch has allowed and encouraged a new generation of collectors to emerge.

Far left: Swatch's 'Pink Pleasure' appeals directly to the young.

Left; The Swatch 'Kishoo'. Only around 150 different designs are introduced each year in four seasonal collection,s and all are limited editions.

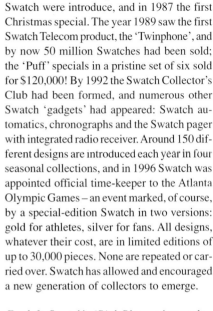

DANIEL ROTH

Founded in 1988, Daniel Roth makes a limited number of watches inspired by four principles: creativity – the Daniel Roth watch has a distinctive profile; integrity – watches crafted meticulously to give precise time-keeping; exclusivity – limited and numbered editions, some as few as 30 pieces; and perfection – an aim difficult to define as well as to achieve. Daniel Roth does not make his own movements, except for *complications*, and it is here that his international reputation lies. His *complications* include a single-face tourbillon and a minute repeater with a perpetual calendar.

ALAIN SILBERSTEIN

More than most, perhaps, the watches of Alain Silberstein are immediately recognisable by

their unique case design and highly individual, brightly coloured dials. But these are no 'pop' watches: they are a serious contribution to art in time-keeping, with top-quality movements, precision metal cases and superbly finished straps and bracelets. Frenchman Silberstein, who is primarily a designer, founded his company in 1989 and concentrates his cases on three shapes: the circle, the square and the triangle, and favours three strong colours: red, yellow and blue. As well as his watches, which are truly collector's pieces, Silberstein designs unique and equally colourful clocks, using traditional French movements.

FRANCK MULLER

Muller started to develop his own designs in 1983, although he did not establish his company until 1991. In the following year, 1984,

Above: Glittering stars from Daniel Roth: 'Lady Diamonds' and 'Lady Diamonds and Rubies'.

Right: A riot of colour in three wristwatches from Alain Silberstein: the perpetual-calendar model, the 'Marine GMT' and the 'Bauhaus Chrono'.

he produced his most complicated watch, which had a *grande* and *petite* strike, minute repeater at hours, quarters and minutes; perpetual calendar programmed to 2100, with day/date mark and monthly equation of time; moon phase; 24-hour indicator; and a thermometer! His inventions are often housed in cases with curved rectangular sides, which he christened the 'Cintree Curvex', and each are usually individual pieces or in limited editions.

GEORGE DANIELS

Dr George Daniels, MBE, FAS, FBHI, is Britain's – some would say the world's – greatest-living horologist, and is the only Englishman in the last 300 years to have made virtually every part of a watch, including cases, hands and engine-turned dials with his own hands. At the rate of one watch every year, for the past 25 years, Daniels doesn't make watches to sell, but to please himself. However, when he has finished one, there is always a buyer waiting, no matter how high the price.

Above: George Daniels at work.

Right: The four-minute tourbillon, with silver dial and coaxial escapement, by George Daniels. Detail: The reverse of the watch, showing the tourbillon. Every part of George Daniel's watches is made in his workshop.

Above: The Franck Muller collection offers an array of forms and complications. From left to right: 'Calibre 95', the distinctive, curved 'Cintree' case and a chronograph.